Contents

Exercise

You need to do some exercise every day.

Exercise keeps your body healthy.

Every day

Do some exercise that makes you breathe fast every day.

You could play chasing games.

Do some exercise that makes your heart beat fast every day.

You could play sports.

You could skip fast.

If you can, stretch before and after you exercise.

Bones

Do some exercise that makes your bones strong.

You could hop or run.

Muscles

Do some exercise that makes your muscles strong.

14

You could try climbing.

Gentle exercise

Gentle exercise helps your body, too.

16

Walk whenever you can.

You could ride on a scooter.

You can even exercise while
you play games.

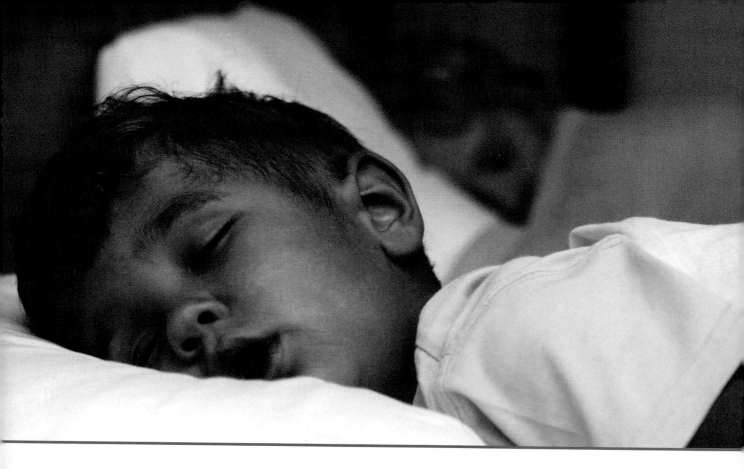

Exercise makes your body strong
and helps you sleep.

Exercise can be fun!

Can you remember?

What should you try to do before and after you exercise?

Answer on page 24

Picture glossary

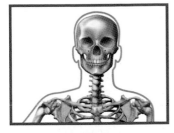

bones you have bones inside your body. Bones help to keep your body up.

muscles stretchy parts inside your body that can make things move

stretch gently pull or push parts of your body

Index

Answer to question on page 22
You should try to stretch before and after exercise.

Notes for parents and teachers

Before reading

Ask the children why exercise is important. Explain that we need to exercise to keep our bodies healthy. Exercise strengthens our bodies and keeps our hearts, muscles, and bones working well. Exercise can even help us to improve our thinking skills and sleep better.

After reading

- Divide the children into pairs and give them time to think about their three favourite ways of exercising. This can include playground games, too. Ask each pair to share their ideas, then group the children into new pairs and ask them to share their ideas again. Did this help them to find other types of exercise that they want to try? If possible, try out some of these together.

- Investigate some of the benefits of exercise with the children. Try holding an early morning exercise session every day for a week. Remind the children of the importance of warming up and cooling down exercises during the session. Reflect upon any benefits the children feel as a result of the exercise and keep a class journal of these.